THE *Symbols* OF EASTER

For Peter, Alina, Cannon,
Pacen, Grace, and James.
All of heaven loves you.

Text © 2018 Rachelle Pace Castor
Cover: *He Loves Me* © 2018 Jon McNaughton
Pages 6–7: *Easter Egg Hunt* © 2018 Ronald Bayens
Page 9: *Love's Pure Light* © 2018 Annie Henrie Nader
Pages 10–11: *He Loves Me* © 2018 Jon McNaughton
Pages 12–13: *Healing His Wings* © 2018 Jon McNaughton
Pages 14–15: *Palm Sunday* © 2018 Kyle Henry
Page 18: *Savior* © 2018 Annie Henrie Nader
Page 21: *Streams of Mercy* © 2018 Annie Henrie Nader
Pages 24–25: *He Is Risen* © 2018 Jon McNaughton
Pages 26–27: *Garden of the Empty Tomb* © 2018 Linda Curley Christensen
Pages 28–29: *Garden Tomb* © 2018 Jon McNaughton
Page 30: *Hope in the Second Coming* © 2018 Del Parson

This is not an official publication of The Church of Jesus Christ of Latter-day Saints. The opinions and views expressed herein belong solely to the author and do not necessarily represent the opinions or views of Cedar Fort, Inc. Permission for the use of sources, graphics, and photos is also solely the responsibility of the author.

ISBN 13: 978-1-4621-2172-4

Published by CFI, an imprint of Cedar Fort, Inc.
2373 W. 700 S., Springville, UT 84663
Distributed by Cedar Fort, Inc., www.cedarfort.com

Library of Congress Cataloging-in-Publication data on file

Cover and interiors designed by Shawnda T. Craig
Cover design © 2018 by Cedar Fort, Inc.
Edited by Kaitlin Barwick

Printed in the United States of America

10 9 8 7 6 5 4 3 2 1

Printed on acid-free paper

THE *Symbols* OF EASTER

RACHELLE PACE CASTOR

CFI
AN IMPRINT OF CEDAR FORT, INC.
SPRINGVILLE, UTAH

Marshmallow chicks and bunnies in rows, eggs of all colors and baskets with bows.

Feed the new lamb and pet the soft bunny, chase yellow ducklings that waddle so funny, for this is Easter time!

Dress in
your best
for the
Easter parade.
Now ready set run—
dont be
afraid!

Fill up your basket.
Search all around.
Then sit
on the grass
and share
what you've found,
for this is
Easter time!

With a chorus
of springtime
tones
in the air,
it seems
Mother Earth
is singing
a prayer.

Rejoicing
in Jesus and life
now renewed,
we too sing
of Easter
with deep
gratitude.

Hunting for *treasures* at
Easter time
brings joy and
delight
when we make a find.

Like searching
the scriptures
to learn what is
true,
each story of
Jesus
has answers for you.

The wind
lifts
colorful kites
way up high,
a symbol of
prayers
rising
into the sky.

God hears
our plea as we hunger
and thirst,
and sends
miracles
when our
faith
is shown first.

We get ready
for Easter
in many ways
as we plan
and create
for that
special day.

Like those
who placed cloth
and waved the
palm leaves,
to honor
Christ best,
our heart must
believe.

The children
all love to
make and share
treats—
a reminder that
Christ
turns bitter to sweet.

He offered
His life for
the whole human race,
gaining power
to save us
through
heavenly grace.

When heaven
and earth
grew dark with sorrow,
some held to
the promise of
hope for tomorrow.

Like a
once-empty
basket
now
brimming
and bright,
our hearts too will brim
with the Savior's
pure light.

Tulips and
lilies
asleep in the earth
await the
spring sunlight
to give them
rebirth.

A symbol of *Jesus*,
who lay in the grave,
soon to awaken,
God's children
to save.

The
Easter Bunny
freely gives
gifts that remind us
Jesus lives.

We too can
give gifts
that share the story
that Christ
has risen
in all His glory.

Tucked in a
chrysalis,
the caterpillar
knows
that soon it will fly
as each wing
forms and grows.

A symbol that
death is
a part of perfection
through Christ's
sacrifice
and His
First Resurrection.

After sleeping
in darkness
without any sight,
ducklings
and chicks
peck their way
to the light.

When someone
we love dies,
we know that
one day
we will see
them again,
for Christ
opened the way.

On Easter,
her tears
fell
like rain
to the ground
when the
emptiness
of His tomb was all
that she found.

"*Mary*," He said,
then she looked
and could see
He had risen.
Hallelujah!
Her Savior was free!

Springtime
is beautiful,
vibrant, and bright.
The earth
regains life from the
Savior's
pure — light.

And all things
bear witness that *Jesus*
now lives.
He lives. Yes, He lives.
Our sweet
Jesus lives.

Lilies, ducklings, chicks, and flowers; butterflies, bunnies, gentle spring showers. Searching for treasures, candy, and eggs; ribbons, and baskets, and Easter parades.

Dressed in our best, we retell the story of Christ's Resurrection in all of His glory.

Springtime is when the whole earth gives testimony that Jesus lives, For this is Easter time!